THE ART OF
MINDFUL DRAWING

ARCTURUS

This edition published in 2016 by Arcturus Publishing Limited
26/27 Bickels Yard, 151–153 Bermondsey Street,
London SE1 3HA

ISBN: 978-1-78599-184-4
AD004925UK

Printed in China

THE ART OF
MINDFUL DRAWING

CREATE CALM AND INSPIRING IMAGES

BARRINGTON BARBER

ARCTURUS

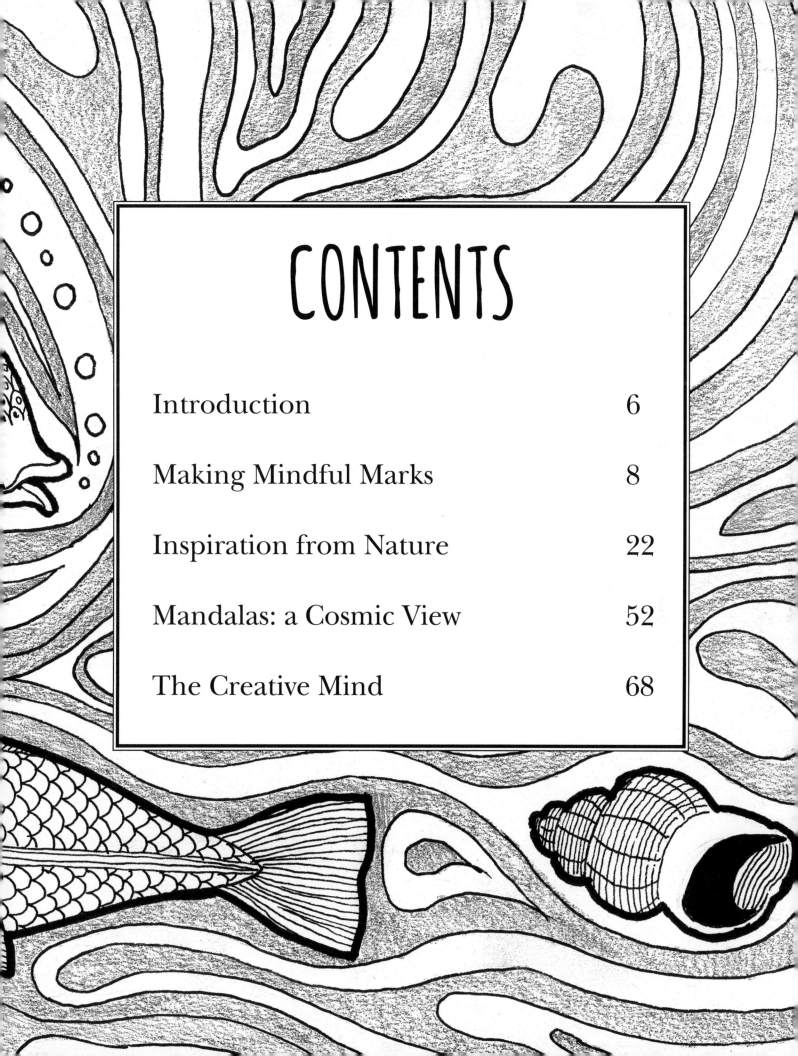

CONTENTS

Introduction   6

Making Mindful Marks   8

Inspiration from Nature   22

Mandalas: a Cosmic View   52

The Creative Mind   68

INTRODUCTION

From this book you will discover the basics of mindful drawing, which will give you the means to concentrate your attention on a simple and stress-free activity – evaluating and describing form and design. With other thoughts put aside, the mind is stilled and calm, allowing you to relax in a form of meditation.

We shall start with some straightforward exercises which train your attention towards observing without worrying about identifiable results. This quiet concentration is a way of calming the overactive mind, which continually tries to alert our consciousness towards every possible thing that will grasp our interest. By using a disciplined method of resting our attention on quite easy but definite exercises, it is possible to shut away this agitated distraction and find a more detached way of observing the activity that we are engaged in. This can bring a calmer, more objective view of what we are doing without making it less interesting – in fact it leads to greater skills in drawing. The passion that an artist feels for engaging his or her skills is balanced out by a certain impartiality, so that he or she can evaluate the effectiveness of the work.

The decorative forms of mandalas and other such motifs are useful because they require both a deep interest in how the design will come out and a very detached ability to just form the shapes without mental comment or criticism. The more you practise drawing while calm of mind, the easier it will become to be inventive and original. Turning off the critical voice in your head will not stop you from being able to improve each shape and mark in such a way that the final effect is more artistic; most good art is the result of careful, intense work.

So, give your artistic, emotional brain some rest and enjoyment by trying out these methods of drawing decorative images, based here on the shapes of nature and geometry. There is nothing in this book that is daunting; you need no more than a few drawing tools, some paper, and a little time.

Barrington Barber

MAKING MINDFUL MARKS

In this chapter you will find a variety of fairly simple exercises in drawing which concentrate on the elementary making of lines and shapes. The aim here is to focus intently on the point of the pencil as it traces out the marks on the surface. These first exercises are about giving your full attention to the making of marks on the paper. That is really what drawing is all about, however much we try to give it other meanings. It is about the process rather than the final result.

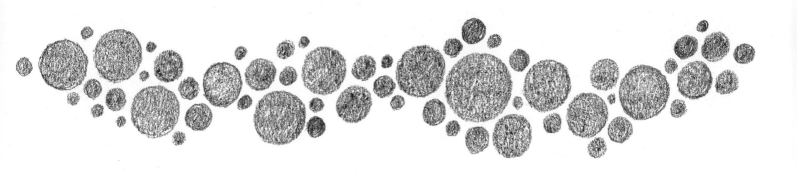

LINES OF THOUGHT

The intention here is not to draw exciting pictures, but simply to make a line as straight as possible without worrying whether the final effect is perfect. Just concentrating your attention on the actual experience should give you confidence in the marks that appear. At first they may not be very well formed, but as you focus on the moving pencil lead you will find your mind stilled and your marks improved.

1. Begin by drawing a series of straight vertical lines, closely spaced and all the same length and distance apart. Give this your full attention and watch the lines appear without too much concern about their perfection – just try to achieve that straightness and simplicity.

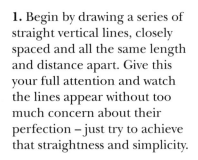

2. Move on to a series of horizontal lines in the same style. You will then have two squares of straight lines in opposite directions. Repeat this exercise until your attention is really focused on your marks and you are content with how they look.

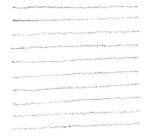

3. Next, draw parallel lines again but this time achieving a square of diagonal marks. This is a bit more challenging as you have to make a decision about how long each line is going to be, rather than just matching the length of the previous one. Draw them in the way that seems easiest to you.

4. Then draw diagonal lines in the opposite direction. Notice how keeping the lines straight is often quite difficult, but don't be concerned – even accomplished artists can find it so. As before, the main effort is to keep your attention directly on where the point of the pencil touches the paper as the lines appear.

5. Now try some more expansive exercises to keep your attention on your pencil. First make a series of vertical zigzags across the page that are all about the same length and the same angle. This should flow naturally after the first few strokes, but don't let your attention wander. Make as many of these as you like until you feel at ease with both the movement and the results.

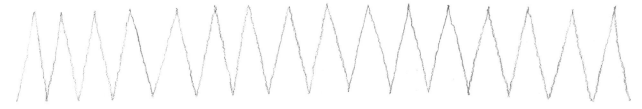

6. The next one is more flowing, with a series of looping curves across the page. Keep the loops as similar as possible and feel how your fingers and wrist allow the shapes to appear fairly easily. Again practise this until the movement is easy and flowing. If your hand or wrist become tense, relax before continuing. There should be as little tension in your body as possible, and in your mind too.

7. Now draw an equilateral triangle – that is, one with all sides the same length. You will probably find you draw them with unequal length at first, but give the exercise your full attention and persist until you feel you have arrived at your goal.

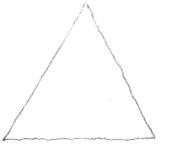

8. Now draw another one, this time the opposite way up. Many people find it easier to draw a triangle one way up than the other and this may be true in your case, but just concentrate and see what happens.

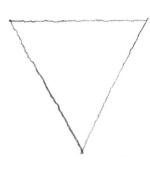

9. Now draw two isosceles triangles opposite ways up. These have two sides the same length and a shorter third one.

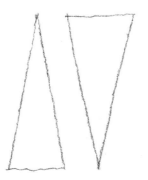

10. Draw two right-angled triangles close together as shown, trying to make them similar in size.

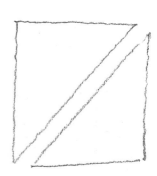

11. You know what a square looks like, but drawing one accurately is quite a test of your sense of shape and proportion. Keep it in your mind while you draw that each side is the same length and all the corners are right angles.

12. When you think your squares are going well, draw a square angled on to its corner, looking like a diamond. It is not quite so easy to get the angles correct.

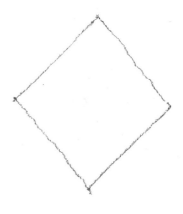

13. Now draw a square with other squares inside it, as many as you can fit in. First draw them at the same angle then start again, this time rotating each one by 90 degrees so you have alternate squares and diamonds.

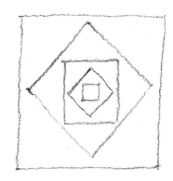

14. This exercise requires skill of both mind and hand to make a complex shape that might easily go awry. Draw a five-angled figure in the shape of a star, which requires you to judge the required angle each time in order to arrive at the classic star shape. Once you've tried it out, you should be able to draw the star in one continuous stroke, gaining speed and fluidity with practice.

15. A six-pointed star is easier as it is just one triangle laid over another.

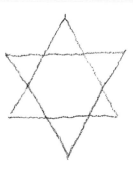

16. An eight-pointed star is also easy, being one square laid over another.

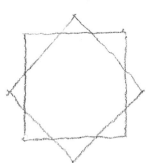

17. A seven-pointed star is trickier, but it is just like the five-pointer with narrower angles. Give it all your attention and make sure you are relaxed in your arms, shoulders and hands.

18. Next, try a nine-pointed star. This may result in a lack of control, which is to a certain extent what we are trying to achieve. Try a few times, concentrating on how your mind and body can work together.

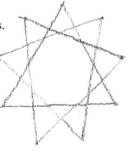

19. Now make a more artistic effort to draw a multi-pointed figure. See if you can produce a recognizable sun shape without drawing anything but the rays.

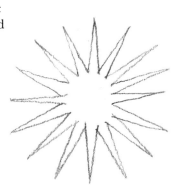

20. This 12-pointed figure is composed of three triangles. Make them as balanced as possible to achieve a good star.

21. As a last bit of careful artistic control, draw two crescents facing each other. Which way round did you find a crescent easier to draw? Work on the more difficult crescent until it comes as easily as the first.

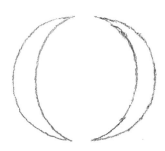

CIRCLES

Circles are good for your drawing practice because it is always possible to improve on your first attempts. Most of us take quite a while to draw a circle freehand with any kind of accuracy. The interesting thing is that it is not difficult to imagine a perfect circle in the mind, but drawing it is something else.

Circles are usually seen to represent unity and wholeness. Infinitely expandable and always exactly curved and centrally based, they are particularly well used in the art of mandalas (see pp.52–67) as all mandalas are circular structures. Geometrically, they are the nearest thing to a perfect form.

1. You have already practised some curving shapes, so now let's concentrate on circles. The first exercise is to try to draw a perfect circle in one or two strokes, without hesitating. Draw rows of circles until you gain some fluency with them. Some people like to draw a circle in one stroke, but I find that two work better for me. Use whichever you find easier.

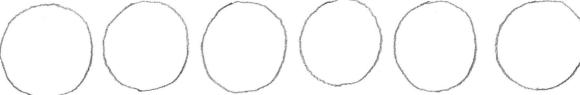

2. So, having drawn a row of circles of a certain size, draw a second row of either larger or smaller ones, trying to make them uniform.

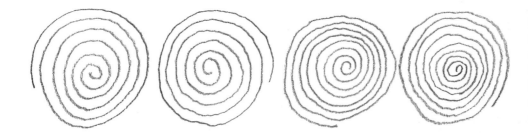

3. Now draw a series of spirals, some starting on the outside working inwards and others starting from the centre. Draw some from left to right and others from right to left. Which arrive most easily and are the most even?

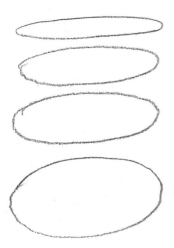

4. Ellipses are the shapes that appear when a circle is seen from an angle, so they are one continuous curve but have one axis longer than the other. Draw them horizontally in different widths across the narrow axis, like you might see if you looked at the top of a glass from different eye levels, then try some vertical ones. Common mistakes are to draw ellipses coming to points or with flattened lines on the wider parts.

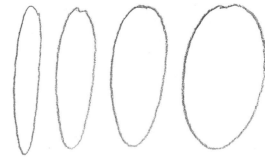

5. Now, back to circles. Draw a large circle filled with smaller ones inside. Try to keep all the small ones about the same size.

6. Visualize a perfect circle in your mind, which is easy enough, then try to draw one. That is a bit more tricky. One way to do it is to draw a circle with a compass and then copy it. Keep erasing and correcting it until, no matter how messy it gets, you start to see something close to a true perfect circle appearing on the paper. This exercise can take quite a bit of time, but persevere until you feel that there is some success.

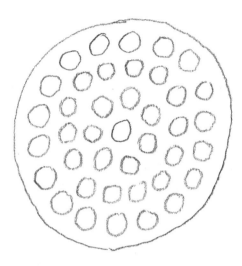
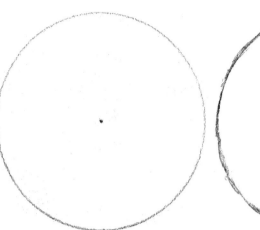
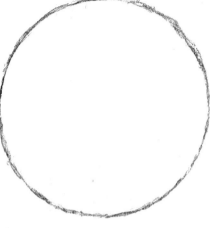

7. Having achieved something more accurate, try a row of smaller circles, all as exact as possible. It's an interesting problem, especially if you attempt to make them all the same size.

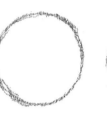

8. Next, carefully draw two ellipses next to each other, with one a bit narrower across its shorter axis but both exactly the same on the longer axis. Draw them with the longer axis both vertical and horizontal.

9. Draw an infinity loop, which is rather like a figure of eight on its side. If you give it two lines to suggest width, what you are drawing is similar to a Mobius strip. This is what you obtain when you take a narrow strip of paper, twist it once and glue the two ends together. What results is a three-dimensional object with only one side and only one edge. Apparently impossible, isn't it? This shape is an example of how images can take us beyond our usual sphere of controlled thought.

CIRCLE PATTERNS

Here are some ideas for how you might combine circles – the beginning of our exploration of pattern. The smaller circles on this page are contained within larger circles and given varying sizes to produce an interesting decorative feature.

First, create two large circles in which to place smaller ones. Use your visual sense to choose where to place larger and smaller inner circles; you will find it comes quite naturally. I shaded in the right-hand circle and you can see this has quite a different effect to the unshaded version.

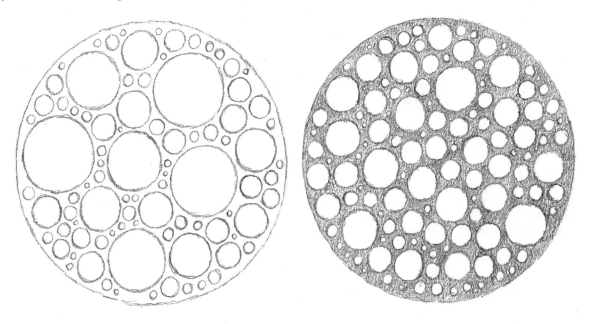

Next, draw several small circles and fill them in with tone. Arrange them across the page like a wandering path of circles.

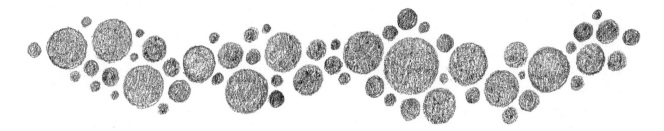

The next example is of a row of circles all the same size but overlapping centre to edge. In the space where the circles overlap, draw some smaller circles as I have done. The uneven row of circles produces a decorative effect as a result of the varying sizes and positions.

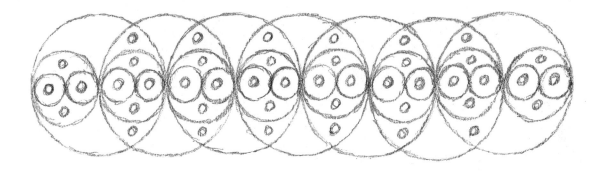

Introducing tone

All the drawing you have done so far has been just with line to indicate shapes. We shall now look at tone, or shading, with which you can give the impression of three dimensions, or solid form. The act of shading will also help you to give your attention to the surface and the marks that you are making upon it.

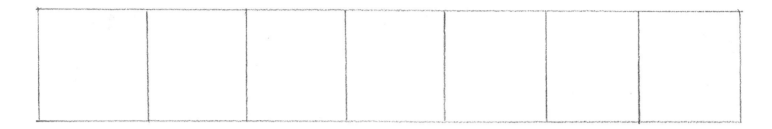

To start with, draw out a set of squares and fill them with pencil marks in a general tone, going from very dark to light or vice versa. Use a soft pencil, at least a B or 2B or even darker. If you start by working from light to dark, leave the first square untouched so that you can see exactly how light your first pencil marks appear. They should be only slightly darker than the empty square. If you start with the darkest square, make it as black as possible and then shade the others gradually lighter.

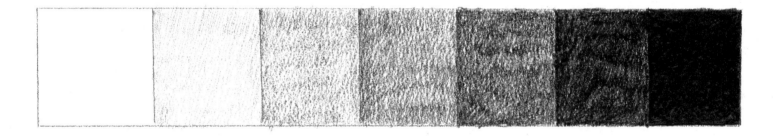

The next exercises explore different ways of producing shading or tone. First draw marks very close together at the angle that you find easiest, aiming for an even tone. Repeat, using vertical strokes, then make a third patch using horizontal strokes.

Next, start with very dark strokes and gradually let them fade to lighter and lighter tones, until the tone disappears.

Return to vertical strokes, but this time make them the whole length of the patch of tone. Then go over them with horizontal strokes, and then diagonal ones in two directions. You should achieve a fairly solid dark tone.

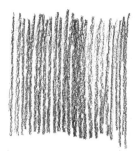 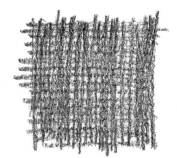 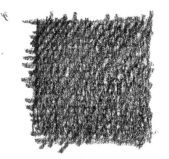 

Now try other methods of making tone, first by very short marks all over the area.

Then make dots over the whole area, as evenly as possible.

Next make an endless weaving line over the whole area until it looks fairly evenly covered.

Make an area of tone, then smudge it with your finger or a paper stump (tortillon). This produces a very diffuse tone.

 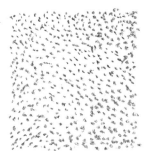 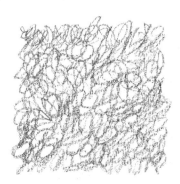 

You will be at ease with drawing quite accurate circles now, but this time add tone to make a two-dimensional circle look like a three-dimensional sphere. Put in a simple light tone over the bottom right-hand side so that it leaves a circular area untouched by tone over about a quarter of the area at the top left-hand side.

Now gradually increase the darkness of the tone away from the light area at the top so that the darkest area of tone is in a crescent just slightly away from the bottom right-hand edge.

To give it more conviction as a spherical object, add a cast shadow at the bottom edge to spread across the apparent surface that the sphere is resting on. The more care and attention you put into this the better the result will look.

Now construct what appears to be a cube. This is done by drawing a flattened diamond shape and then extending three vertical lines of equal length from the upper three corners of the shape and joining them with two angled lines between. Make sure that the angle of the lower lines is the same as the two corresponding upper ones.

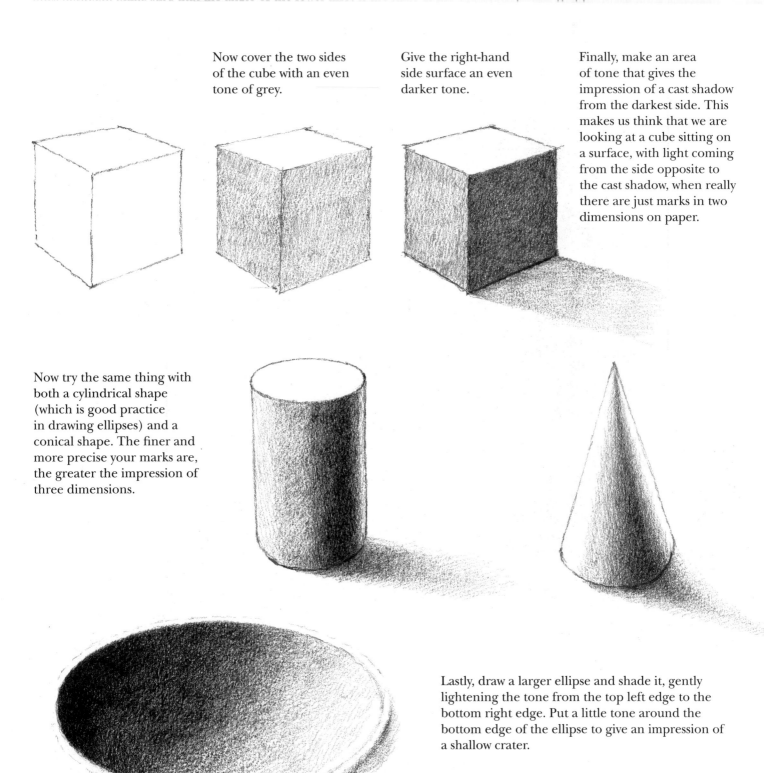

Now cover the two sides of the cube with an even tone of grey.

Give the right-hand side surface an even darker tone.

Finally, make an area of tone that gives the impression of a cast shadow from the darkest side. This makes us think that we are looking at a cube sitting on a surface, with light coming from the side opposite to the cast shadow, when really there are just marks in two dimensions on paper.

Now try the same thing with both a cylindrical shape (which is good practice in drawing ellipses) and a conical shape. The finer and more precise your marks are, the greater the impression of three dimensions.

Lastly, draw a larger ellipse and shade it, gently lightening the tone from the top left edge to the bottom right edge. Put a little tone around the bottom edge of the ellipse to give an impression of a shallow crater.

SHADING WITH A DIFFERENCE

As you discovered on the previous pages, all sorts of different marks can be used to create tone, from hatching and cross-hatching to tiny circles, dots or even zigzags. Here, each circle was first drawn with a compass and then shaded in with varying marks to act as tone, always leaving the upper area on the left lighter, to give the impression that it is a spherical object (a ball).

You can have a lot of fun with this exercise, while improving your dexterity and shading technique.

THE POSSIBILITIES OF PATTERN

Here are a few ideas to demonstrate the drawing of patterns, which are quite easy and come naturally to most people. Patterns are a very ancient method of producing decoration by the simple repetition of shapes over a uniform area. Most can be created by dividing up a space uniformly and then fitting various simple shapes into each space, alternating the shapes to create more interest. You will find examples of this sort of patterning all around you, even for example in brickwork where the bricks are laid in a herringbone design.

A very simple example is to place a series of spots or small circles across a field. They could be either aligned in some way or purely random.

This series of wave shapes is very uniform and vertical in form. Use lines to make a texture effect between them.

Next are rows of small circles or spots alternating with diamond squares with a spot inside them.

Dividing the area into squares and filling some with broad crosses, tone or just a line gives a geometric, ordered pattern.

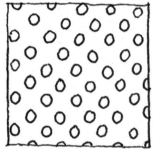  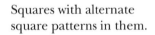 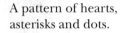 

Curved lines crossed by zigzags.

Squares with alternate square patterns in them.

A mix of stars and crescents.

A pattern of hearts, asterisks and dots.

1. Repetition and geometry are pleasing to the eye, and stripes are the most simple form of this.

2. Fill the stripes with semi-circles on alternate strips.

3. Then fill in with some tone and put stars and spots in the empty stripes.

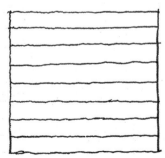 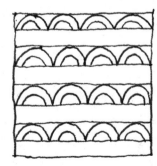 

So far we have been looking at patterns with a geometric feel. However, you will find much to inspire you in organic, natural shapes and textures.

Watery lines across the space.

Large lightning flashes.

Another suggestion of water, this time oily, with a vertical influence.

Flame-like shapes.

Wave-shaped lines, moving horizontally.

In the next chapter we shall be taking this exploration of natural forms further to see how you can use nature as the basis of your mindful drawing.

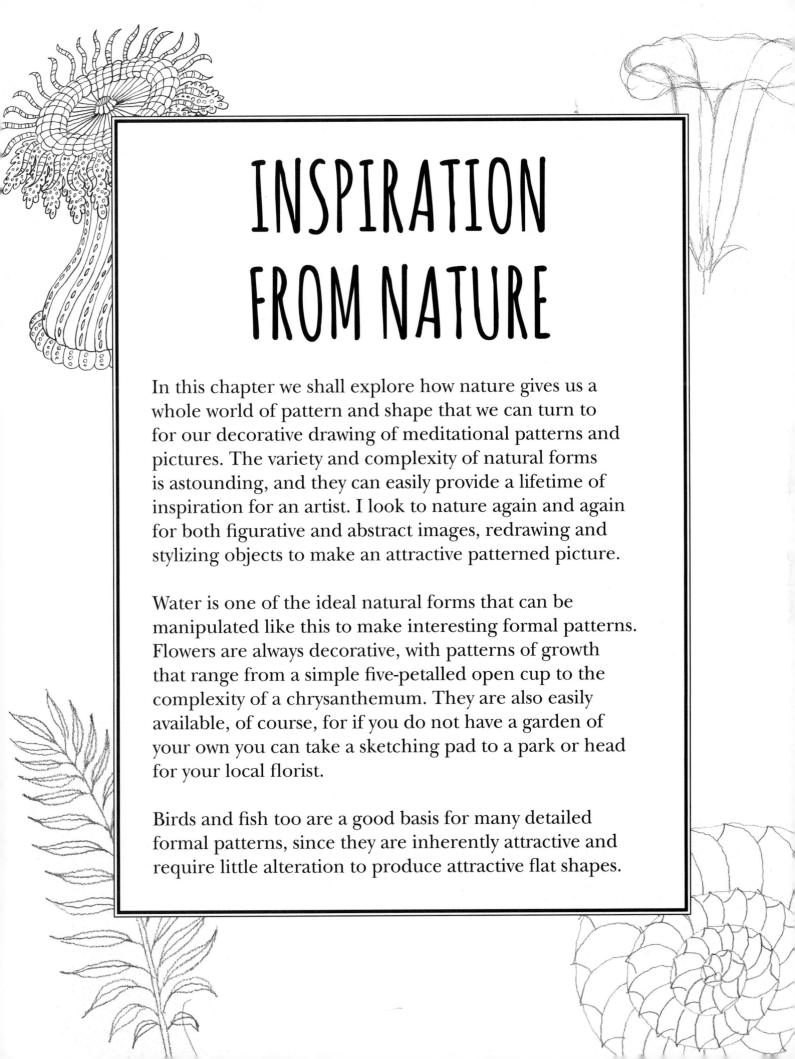

INSPIRATION FROM NATURE

In this chapter we shall explore how nature gives us a whole world of pattern and shape that we can turn to for our decorative drawing of meditational patterns and pictures. The variety and complexity of natural forms is astounding, and they can easily provide a lifetime of inspiration for an artist. I look to nature again and again for both figurative and abstract images, redrawing and stylizing objects to make an attractive patterned picture.

Water is one of the ideal natural forms that can be manipulated like this to make interesting formal patterns. Flowers are always decorative, with patterns of growth that range from a simple five-petalled open cup to the complexity of a chrysanthemum. They are also easily available, of course, for if you do not have a garden of your own you can take a sketching pad to a park or head for your local florist.

Birds and fish too are a good basis for many detailed formal patterns, since they are inherently attractive and require little alteration to produce attractive flat shapes.

SIMPLIFYING FLOWER FORMS

Here are a series of designs, mostly based on a circle shape, that you can adapt into effective flower-like forms. All blossoms have a relatively simple basic shape, with small differences that identify the particular type of flower. In the example start with a diagrammatic version and then make a drawing with more precision and flower-like textures.

1. Draw a circle. From the central point draw five large loops that touch the edge of the circle and finish back at the centre. The loops should overlap slightly. Draw a small circle around the central point.

2. Now draw the outline of the overlapping petals with some simple marks to suggest texture. Draw some stamens radiating outwards from the centre and little points of leaf where the petals overlap.

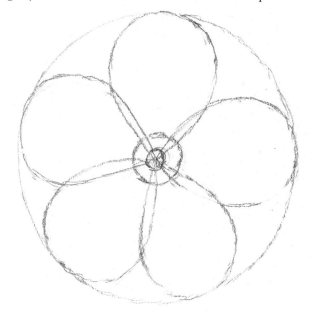

1. Now draw a similar pattern with six overlapping heart-shaped petals.

2. Firm up the outline, showing the overlap on one side only and put in some small circle-like shapes to denote the centre of the flower.

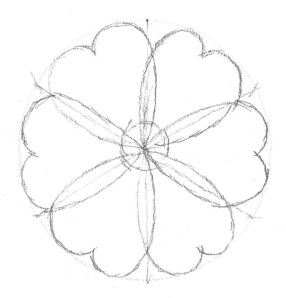

1. For this next pattern, draw two circles, one inside the other, as I have done. From the inner circle draw a number of narrow petals with curved ends, their tips touching the outer circle. Draw lots of small circles in the centre of your flower design.

2. Now firm up your shapes, making the petal shapes more natural-looking and the flower centre quite dense with lots of small scribbly circles. The pattern resembles a sunflower.

1. Draw a set of four concentric circles. Around the central point and the three inner circles draw five curves to denote petals: the petals will be smaller towards the centre. Draw small pointed leaf shapes between the outermost petals.

2. When you formalize the pattern, add extra edges to the petal shapes to suggest a curved edge. This pattern has the look of a Tudor rose.

1. From the centre of a circle draw seven overlapping petal shapes, this time tapering to a point where they touch the circle's edge. Draw

2. Firm up the lines and add some detail in the centre to resemble stamens.

1. Draw an ellipse. Then draw a set of long petals in a cone shape, extending up and curving over the edge of the ellipse.

2. Now draw it all more firmly and put in some tall stamens and the stalk from which this lily-shaped flower grows. With the addition of some simple shading, this design starts to look quite realistic.

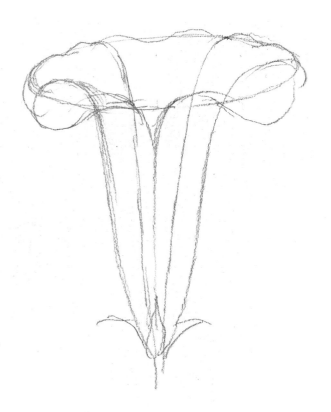

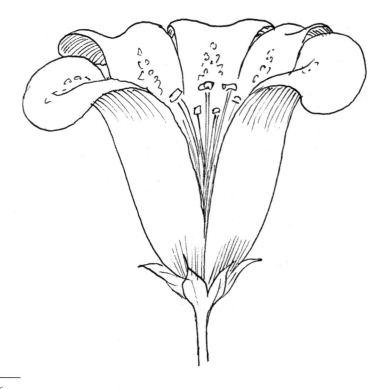

Iris

Now we move on to some more detailed drawings. The aim is once again to observe, draw and simplify the flower shapes.

STEP 1

The iris is a very formal flower in structure, so it will not present a problem for the artist wishing to make it into a pattern. The naturalistic drawing is already quite decorative. This is your starting point, where you set out to describe the shapes, textures and tones of the plant. Don't worry if your drawing is not as realistic as mine; the idea is to familiarize yourself with the flower and its form, not to make a perfect rendition.

STEP 2

Next, draw a more simplified version to show the main shape and texture.

STEP 3

Finally, make a slightly more formal version that retains the shape and feel of the original flower but eliminates the irregularities found in nature.

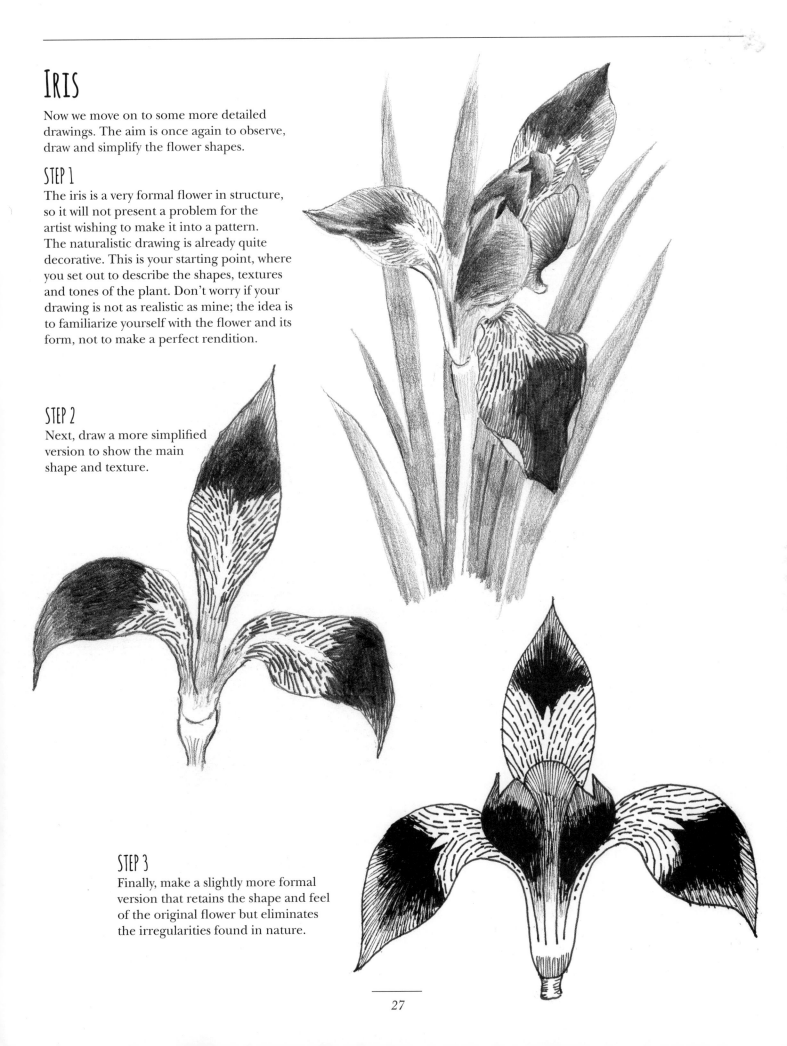

Clematis

A winter-flowering species, *Clematis cirrhosa* has small, delicate flowers that will make an interesting basic shape for a pattern.

STEP 1
First make a drawing of the flower as it is in reality, as naturally as possible.

STEP 2
Then draw a carefully outlined version, formalizing the shapes and textures.

STEP 3
Reduce the flowers to just two and further formalize the arrangement.

STEP 4
Finally, make an even more simplified version of the flowers, which can be used as a motif for decoration.

FLOWER WREATH

Having drawn the formalized version of the two flowers,
it is easy enough to arrange them into a circle to create a
floral wreath. I have shown it with the leaves on the inside
but it can equally be done in reverse with
the flowers facing inwards.

Holly sprig

The holly sprig was in reality a five-leaved entity, but I have reduced it to three leaves only and three berries. This makes it very easy to arrange for any kind of repetition that covers as large an area as you think fit. I have shown it as a sort of paving with alternating sprigs of lighter and darker berries. Where the berries are lighter, I have darkened the leaves behind them to make them stand out more.

EUPHORBIA

As with some of the other flowers, this *Euphorbia stygiana* is rather formal in shape already so the two steps to a complete formalization are easy to see. In the very last version the leaves and centre are made very balanced and regular.

1

2

3

This reduced view of a euphorbia is now quite easy to repeat ad infinitum to produce patterns.

AUTUMN LEAVES

This leaf, found on the grass in my local park, had fallen from the tree and was a quite deep reddish colour. Unlike many autumn leaves it had stayed flat, which meant that it was much easier to draw.

Then it was just a matter of alternating the leaf shape, sometimes stalk down and sometimes stalk up, to make a pattern. The dark tracing of the veins is emphasized by the white outlines around them. To make a more complex pattern, you could repeat the two shapes in a tessellation.

FERN FRONDS

1

2

3

Ferns have beautiful, delicate fronds that unfurl from the centre of the plant. You can produce these fern-like shapes by first constructing the basis as shown, and then adding the repetitive leaf shapes in various ways to evoke interesting patterns.

TREES

Trees are a true wonder of nature; they can live for hundreds and in some cases even thousands of years, they provide a habitat for a whole raft of insects and animals and they convert carbon dioxide gas into breathable oxygen. In these drawings I tried to get a sense of the whole living, breathing organism by including the roots below ground. This gives the compositions a sense of balance and makes them more decorative, as the shapes of the roots mirror the branches above.

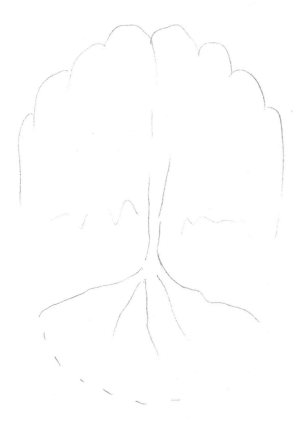

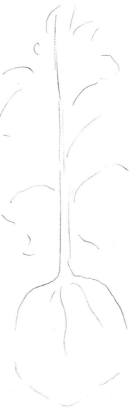

STEP 1

The two trees can be drawn in a faint outline at first to help you decide exactly how large they should be and the number of branches you wish to include in the finished drawing.

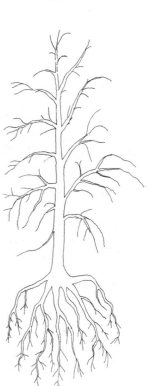

STEP 2

Having done this, draw the whole basic shape rather more carefully, deciding how the branches will grow out into many twigs and the thick roots into fine, hair-like tendrils. Make sure on both trees that the roots are large enough to look balanced.

The willow tree needs to be drawn rather less finalized, so mark the drooping masses of leaves without yet defining them too exactly.

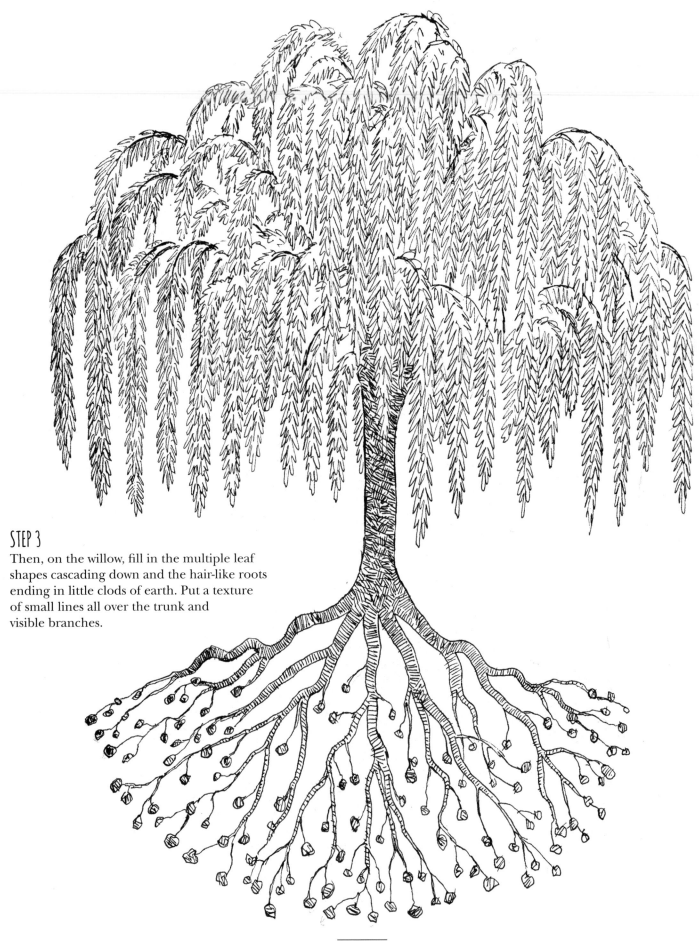

STEP 3

Then, on the willow, fill in the multiple leaf
shapes cascading down and the hair-like roots
ending in little clods of earth. Put a texture
of small lines all over the trunk and
visible branches.

STEP 3

On the straighter tree, mark in small leaves all over the twigs and branches and fill in the trunk with small lines to give it the look of bark. As in the willow, put small clods of earth at the ends of the smallest roots.

SHELLS AND SEA ANEMONES

Here are some shell and sea anemone shapes which are already decorative in their natural state. All you need to do is treat them simply as line drawings, using the striations on the surfaces for their patterns. My drawings are based on the amazing work of naturalist and artist Ernst Haeckel in his 1904 work *Art Forms of Nature*.

STEP 1

First, draw the outlines and inner contours, keeping your line as steady and fluid as you can. A large part of the attraction of these objects is their perfect curves, so it is a good idea to practise making these lines first to get your hand in.

STEP 2

Next, draw in their striations, noting how the shell patterns repeat in diminishing size towards the centre.

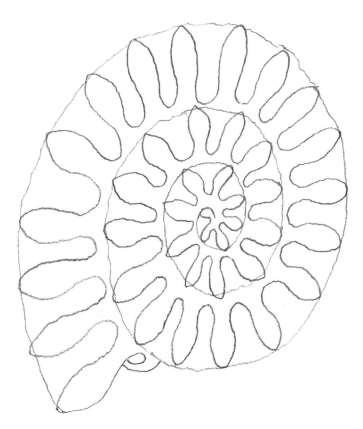

STEP 3

To finish, formalize the patterning – you will see there are a range of marks, including circles, straight and curved lines and zigzags. You may wish to work in pen at this stage as I have done, and erase your original pencil drawing.

STEP 1
Draw the main spiral shape of the shell.

STEP 2
Then put in the sharp-ended curved shapes, from small in the centre to large on the shell's outer edge.

STEP 3
As before, erase your guidelines. Finally add the finer patterning of the shell to denote texture. I've used small curves and zigzags.

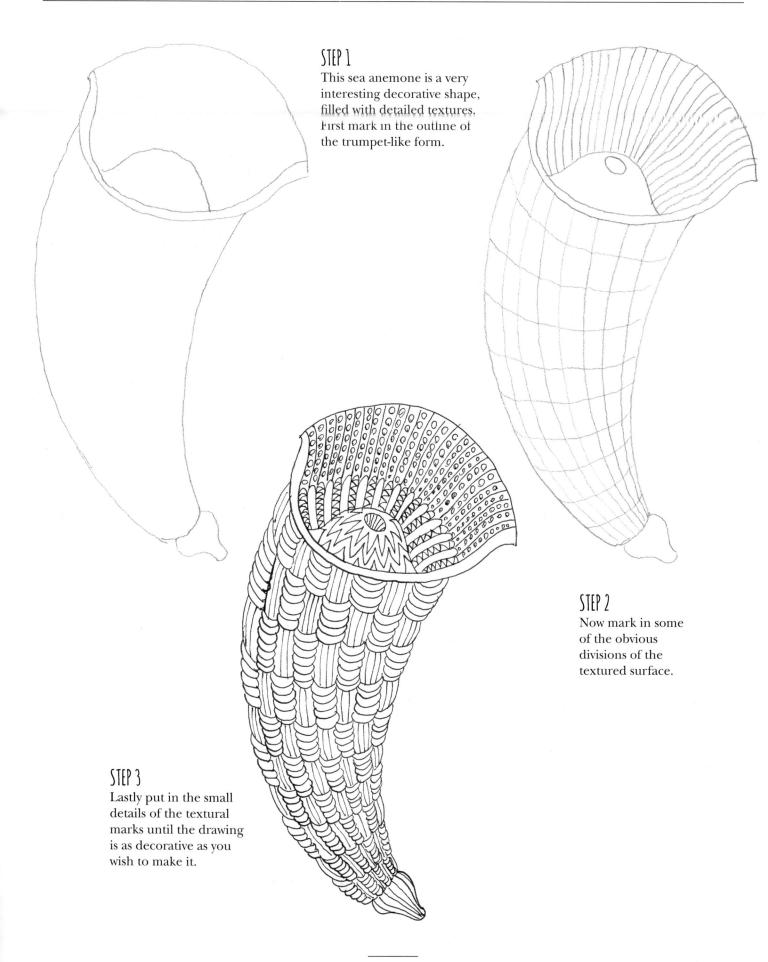

STEP 1
This sea anemone is a very interesting decorative shape, filled with detailed textures. First mark in the outline of the trumpet-like form.

STEP 2
Now mark in some of the obvious divisions of the textured surface.

STEP 3
Lastly put in the small details of the textural marks until the drawing is as decorative as you wish to make it.

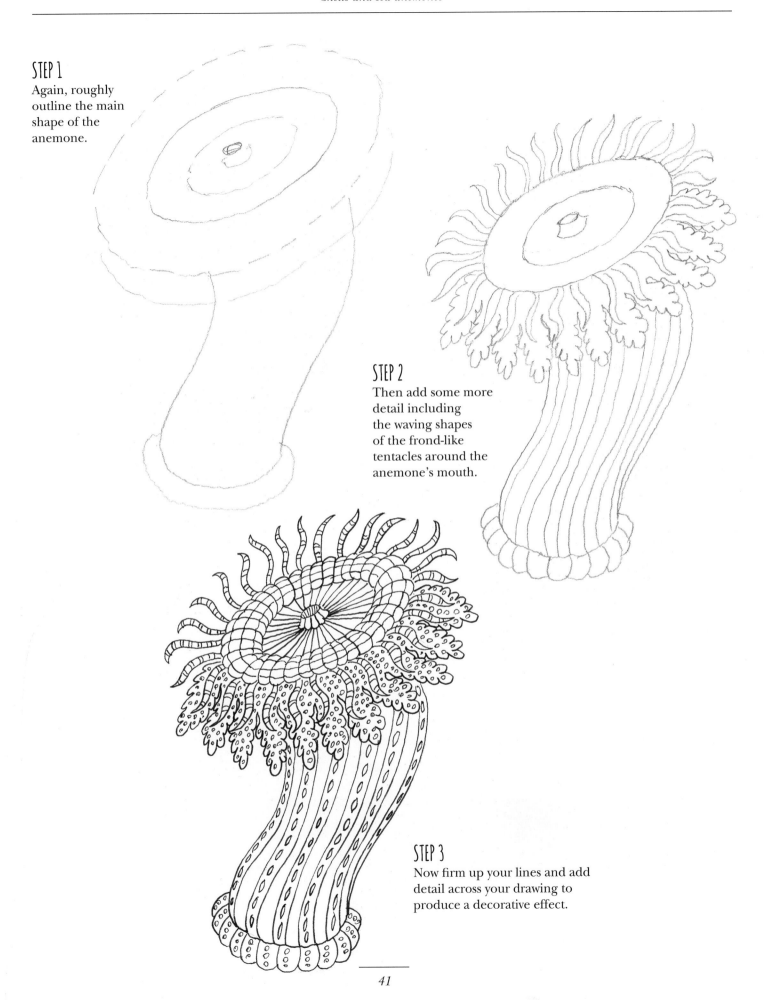

STEP 1
Again, roughly
outline the main
shape of the
anemone.

STEP 2
Then add some more
detail including
the waving shapes
of the frond-like
tentacles around the
anemone's mouth.

STEP 3
Now firm up your lines and add
detail across your drawing to
produce a decorative effect.

WATER PATTERNS

The main problem where drawing water is concerned is that it never stays still. There is always some movement across the surface caused by current, tides or the action of the wind on the surface.

However, when you observe water closely, you will find that many repetitive patterns continually reappear. Your job is to get a feel for how these could be drawn; there is no need to worry if your final result is not something that you can actually see at any one moment. The aim is to watch the way the shapes change but repeat themselves, until you have a clear idea of how the water looks generally. Then draw that as well as you can.

WAVES AT SEA

STEP 1

I took a photograph of sea waves breaking on the shore. Using this as a basis, I did a careful drawing of them with tone and line.

STEP 2

I then carefully simplified the forms of the waves, putting in textures of tone and line where I thought it was necessary.

STEP 3

Next I redefined the shapes even more precisely so that what was a tonal study became a patterned system of shapes resembling the waves of the sea. As you can see, the final patterns are quite definite and formal.

The other two versions were done in exactly the same way, but as the shapes were a bit different I arrived at a different pattern. As before, I began with the natural drawing.

I approached the wave shapes in a similar way, simplifying and defining the various patterns so that they could be turned into decorative pictures.

Snowflakes

The patterns of snowflakes are relatively easy to formalize, even if you can't see any right at this moment. Just remember that they are always six-sided in form and that no two snowflakes are ever exactly the same, then you will be able to design a series of shapes that are snowflake in form, as I have done. You can have a lot of fun here, making the patterns as intricate as you like.

STEP 1
Draw a circle.

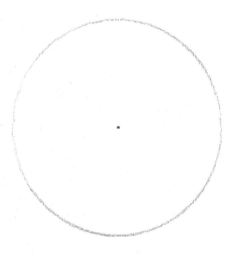

STEP 2
Measure the radius of your circle. Starting at the top of your circle, use the measurement to make six points around the circle.

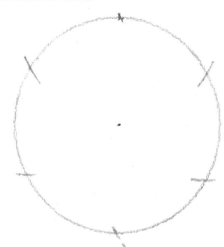

STEP 3
Join each point on the circumference to the centre to divide your circle into six equal parts.

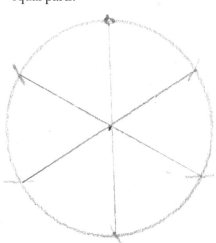

Using your template you can create a myriad of patterns that repeat in each segment of the circle.

You can also try creating white snowflakes on a dark background to see how effective they are. This can be done either by drawing in white paint, crayon or ink on a black surface, or by making a reverse (negative) photocopy of your original drawings.

Rock patterns

Choosing rocks as a subject has the advantage that you know they are not going to move, so you can study them at some length. One thing to notice in particular is the abstract textures and shapes that appear most typical of that type of stone.

The overall texture is quite important as this will give a clear idea about the appearance of any type of rock. The way the rock breaks around the edges also helps to give a form that is recognizable. Look for these aspects and find ways to draw them effectively.

STEP 1
Take a couple of varied pieces of rock, as I have done, and draw them as carefully as you can, showing the shape and texture clearly.

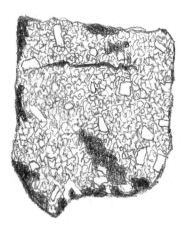 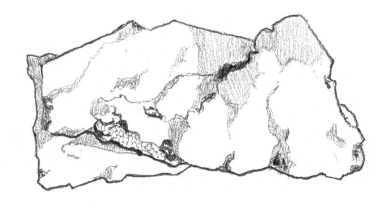

STEP 2
Then draw a more formalized version, keeping the texture but simplifying it and heightening the contrast between light and dark.

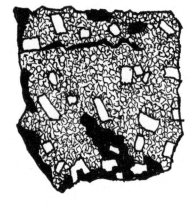 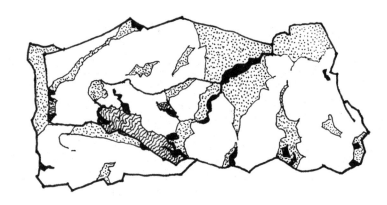

STEP 3
Now alternate the two simplified forms in a grid-like style to build up a rock-pattern design.

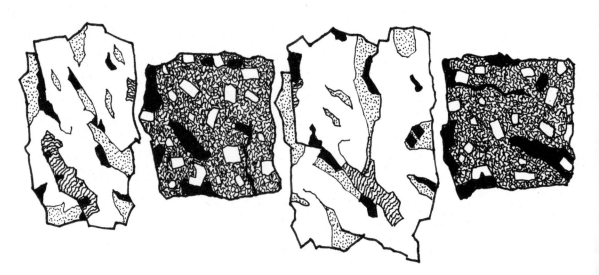

A duck in the water

This drawing is another way of using an interestingly patterned creature as a subject. Here the definition of the patterns is taken further, making a very decorative picture from a natural form.

STEP 1

For reference, I used a photograph of a duck and drew it in as much detail as possible, showing the pattern and texture of the feathers and bill.

STEP 2

Then I redrew it, tracing the shapes and drawing all the textures of the feathers in a deliberately flat patterned way.

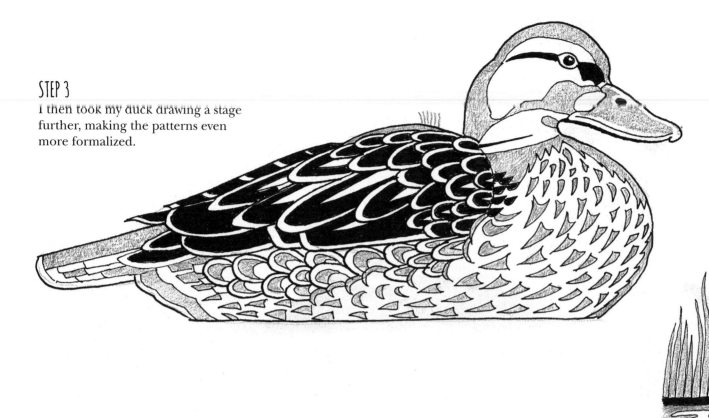

STEP 3

I then took my duck drawing a stage further, making the patterns even more formalized.

STEP 4

Reaching my final goal, I drew around the shape of the duck with patterns that resemble water ripples and reeds. I gave some of the outline shapes a heavier line to emphasize them in parts.

MANDALAS: A COSMIC VIEW

Mandalas are intended to be a decorative and symbolic representation of the cosmos. Usually based on a circular form, they tend to be seen as radiating out from the centre, which is often contained within a square. They are often used as aids to meditation, allowing the onlooker to view the pattern as a sort of shortcut to the universal experience. If the shape and pattern are effective in their design, people find that it is easy to focus their attention on the mandala and block out anything that might intrude on meditative thoughts; the most successful ones have lasted for thousands of years and are still used today.

So, our aim here is to discover how, with careful consideration and an understanding of design, we can produce a harmonious shape, with the pattern radiating outwards.

Mandala template

This set of concentric circles with 24 radial divisions, produced with the aid of a compass and ruler, is the basis for most of the mandalas shown in this chapter. Given the large number of divisions around the circle, it is easy to work out many different designs.

To make this initial construction, first draw a circle using your compass. Measure the length of the radius and use the measurement to make six points around the circumference of your circle. Join these points to the centre point to divide the circle into six equal parts. Then divide these parts in half and then halve them again to make 24 equal segments. Then, within the circle, inscribe several more smaller circles around the same central point; here I have used seven inner circles but this may vary according to your mandala design.

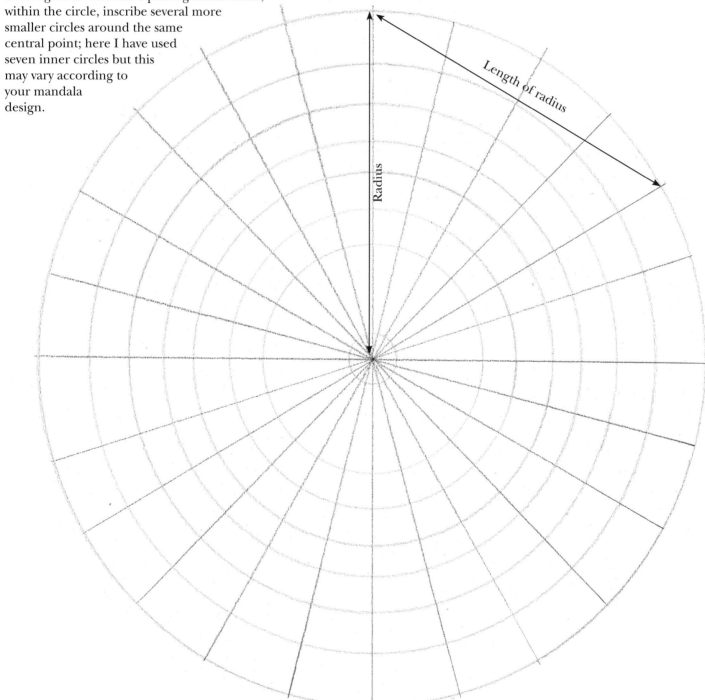

Simple flower mandala

STEP 1

To construct this mandala, draw the template provided on page 54. Then, in the inner circle, make a sunburst pattern along these divisions. Next, put in the curves of the petal shapes around the outside and from the fourth circle in.

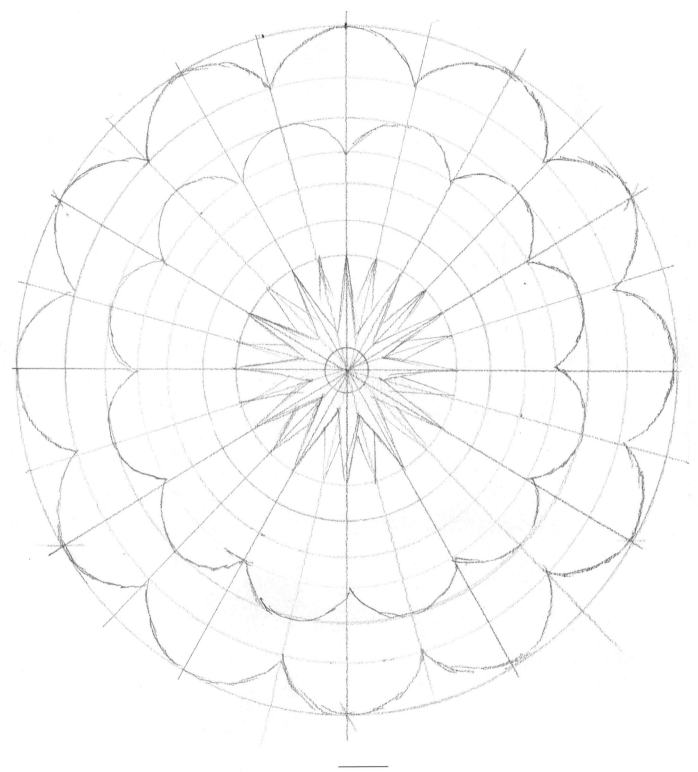

STEP 2

Beneath the upper curve of the petals, add curving lines that dip towards the centre, suggesting curled edges to the petals. Elaborate on the smaller details of the pattern as shown here, with circles, semi-circles and zigzag lines.

DETAILED FLOWER MANDALA

Here is another example of a mandala that you can draw, this time adding more detail to the final design. The larger you draw your template, the more detail you will be able to add to the mandala. Here I intend to develop a floral theme again, though from a template like this there are infinite possibilities you can explore.

STEP 1

On your template, draw two overlapping six-pointed stars, between the inner circle and the penultimate outer circle.

STEP 2

Using tracing paper over your template, draw freehand the decorative shapes of the rose-like creation. Alternatively, you can draw on to your template and erase the guidelines once you are happy with your pattern.

STEP 3

Draw the main shapes in a thicker line and the details in a thinner line. To get good definition you can use a graphic pen over your pencil design; here I used two pens with nibs of 0.5mm and 0.1mm. Working freehand gives a more naturalistic look to the final result.

Om symbol mandala

Om, or Aum, is the nearest English spelling of the sound which in the Indian Hindu mythology is the first word of creation. It also appears in Buddhism and Jainism. The Sanskrit symbol for Om, which is found in ancient scripts, is written with a calligraphic pen, but the angle is opposite to the regular Roman calligraphic pen. To draw the symbol, you can use a regular square-tipped pen or marker and tilt it in the direction you need. Shown below are the steps to produce it.

1. First curve

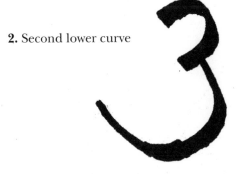

2. Second lower curve

3. Third sideways curve and loop

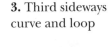

4. Last small curve and dot

To finish, I have drawn an outline around the shape.

STEP 1

The set of concentric circles with the 24 radial divisions detailed on page 54 is the simple basis for my Om mandala. The main part of this mandala is a design to produce a multi-petalled lotus flower shape to enclose the Om symbol. Outside the central circle draw circles of petals alternating, then a circle of sun rays and then the outer petalled circle.

STEP 2

At this stage I added detail to the design with an extra circle of petals and more tightly packed sun rays.

STEP 3

Fill in extra petals and inner shapes in each row of petals, as shown. Then draw in the Om symbol and fill its background area with small circles.

YIN AND YANG MANDALA

This mandala is based on the yin and yang symbol of the ancient philosophy of Taoism. The concept is that in everything there is also its opposite, with an endless process of transference between the two as each reaches its peak and dies back.

1. To draw the inner core of this mandala, make a circle and then two smaller circles within it along the length of the diameter.

2. Draw smaller circles in their centres and then erase the alternate halves of the previous circles to create the yin-yang symbol.

3. Finally, block in tone as shown.

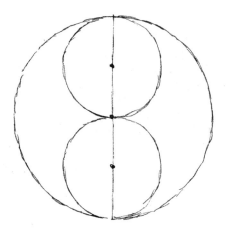

These groups of three lines or trigrams also form part of the Taoist cosmology. To produce them as I have here, draw them all the same thickness and length, then make divisions as shown: three undivided, three with one lower bar divided, one with middle bar divided, one with upper bar divided. Then one with upper and lower bar divided, one with two upper bars divided, one with two lower bars divided, and the last with all three bars divided.

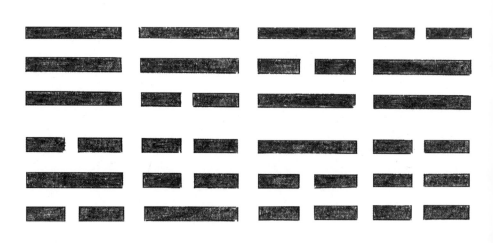

STEP 1

Within a large circle, put six inner circles towards the centre, so that you can mark in all the pattern as shown. Put the yin-yang symbol in the centre and indicate the trigrams around the next division.

Outside this, make wave-like shapes facing outwards. The outer division of the circle can be a series of 24 curved sections as shown.

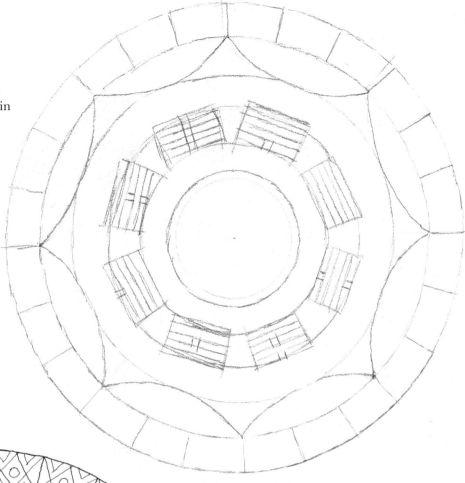

STEP 2

Put the trigrams in more strongly and rub out your guidelines. Draw a second line on the 'waves' and fill in with lines pointing to the outer circle section. In that, draw zigzag lines and circles as shown.

STEP 3

With the main shape and patterns established, block in the
designs with black ink or pencil tone. In some places I have used
a dotted texture to vary the tones of the mandala.

Senses mandala

For the images of the senses in this mandala you will need to make simple drawings of the main sense receivers – the ear, the hand, the eye, the tongue and the nose, signifying hearing, touching, seeing, tasting and smelling.

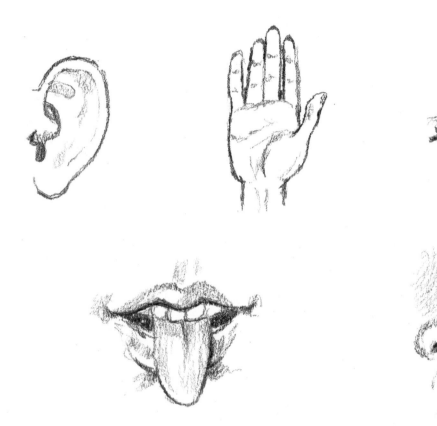

When you have a reasonable image of all these, formalize them by simplification so that they will fit in with the main pattern of the mandala.

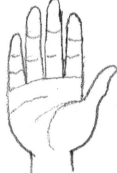

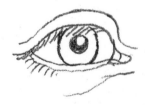

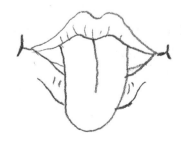

STEP 1

As before, use the radial length of your circle to mark in six points around the circumference. On each of these marks on the circumference, draw overlapping circles all around the base circle. Then draw in smaller circles to fit in the outer section of each of the outer circles, and then one in the centre.

STEP 2

Now add further circular lines to create a more complex and decorative pattern. Add little leaf tips to the outside as shown.

STEP 3

Finally, add in further detail, including the images that represent the senses. You can firm up your design by drawing over it in pen, then rubbing out any stray pencil marks.

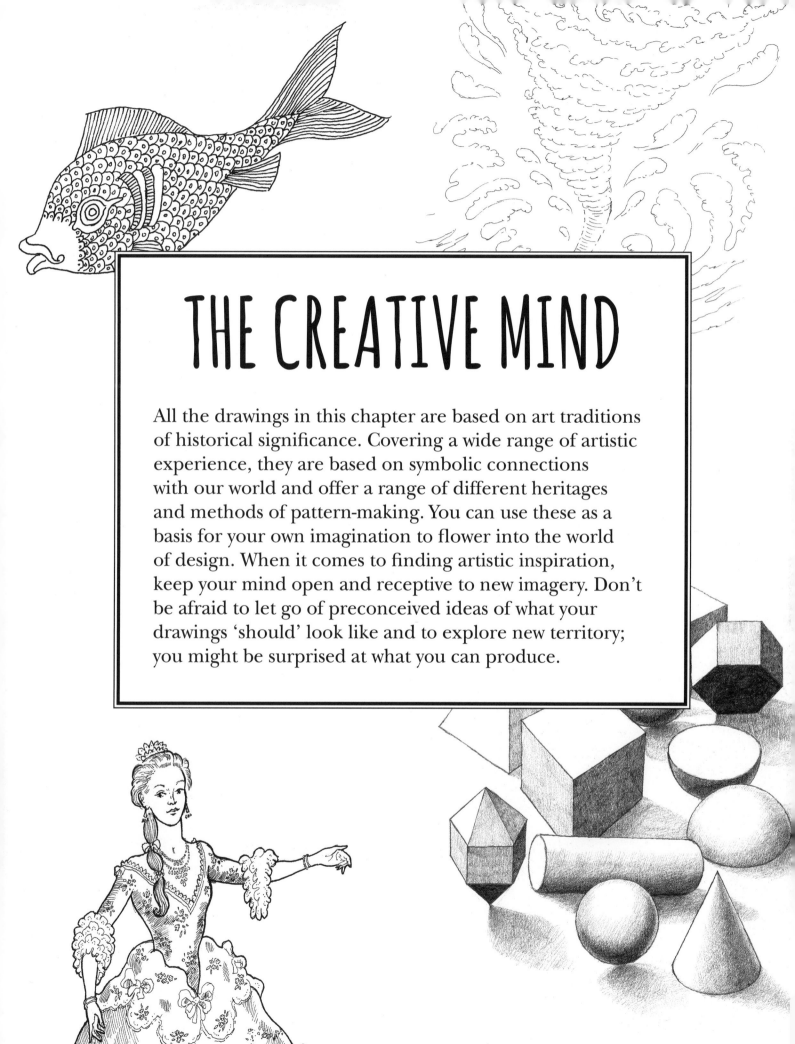

THE CREATIVE MIND

All the drawings in this chapter are based on art traditions of historical significance. Covering a wide range of artistic experience, they are based on symbolic connections with our world and offer a range of different heritages and methods of pattern-making. You can use these as a basis for your own imagination to flower into the world of design. When it comes to finding artistic inspiration, keep your mind open and receptive to new imagery. Don't be afraid to let go of preconceived ideas of what your drawings 'should' look like and to explore new territory; you might be surprised at what you can produce.

Finding inspiration: three iconic images

These three figures from historic sources are typical of the strong decorative tradition of artistic forms. The emperor is from the Byzantine Empire, which was the eastern part of the Roman Empire, centred around Constantinople. The image is taken from a mosaic on one of the buildings in the city.

The Chinese figure is a painting from manuscripts dating from the dynastic times of the old Chinese empire, again drawn in a very detailed, decorative style, while the young princess figure is from the tradition of 18th-century paintings of aristocratic fashionable women of the period.

All these figures lend themselves to the sort of drawing that has great decorative intensity and attraction.

Byzantine emperor

STEP 1
First draw a rough outline version of the figure, dressed in a cloak and crown and a long robe, with one hand gesturing outwards and the other holding a scroll.

STEP 2
Then draw a more accurate outline version, putting in all the main parts of the figure clearly.

STEP 3
Lastly, work over the whole drawing, with plenty of intricate patterning on the clothes.

Lady in a ball gown

Step 1
Once again, draw in the main shape quite lightly and loosely to get some idea of how the figure will look on the page.

Step 2
Draw in the main outline shape more carefully, making sure you have all the main parts of the dress and figure accurately rendered.

Step 3
Now go to town with bows and little flower patterns all over the dress. Add a little tonework in lines that will make the material of the dress look a bit silky and shimmery.

Magnificent mandarin

Step 1
Draw in the main shape lightly first.

Step 2
Next draw up the figure with more detail and accuracy, getting all the main areas marked out clearly.

Step 3
Lastly, take your time filling in the detail and texture of Chinese-looking patterns and decoration.

Medieval building: Florence Sacristy

This iconic building in the cathedral square in Florence, Italy, is one I have always admired, with its brilliant marbled surface of dark lines on light stone. I thought it would be a good way of showing how to produce a similar decorative feature.

I have drawn it in situ, but this particular drawing is from a photograph that I took one year when showing people around the artistic beauties of Florence.

STEP 1

The first step here is a direct copy of the photograph, showing the design as clearly as possible.

STEP 2

The next step is to draw it
more diagrammatically to
simplify the effect of
the patterning.

STEP 3

The last step is to use the same kind of patterning, but a flat rectangular version of it. This does not pretend to be a building, just a decorative architectural surface. Any other period of architecture could be worked over in the same way.

PERSIAN MINIATURE TREE

This drawing of a decorative version of a tree is from an old Persian miniature painted in great detail in manuscript form. I have made a fairly accurate copy of the image with all the tremendous detail shown. It has a similar quality to the wonderful Persian carpets that come from the same tradition.

STEP 1

To start with, draw out the tree shape simply to form the main part of the tree and adjacent potted plants.

STEP 2

Next, carefully draw an outline shape as precisely as you can, allowing areas where some leaves and birds may appear in the picture.

STEP 3

Now put in some of the largest blossoms and the birds in the branches. Try to keep your overall composition balanced.

STEP 4

Complete the outline including all the leaves and birds in the branches.

STEP 5

Finally, fill in all the details of patterning
to produce a decorative effect,
similar to a Persian
miniature painting
of a tree.

SYMBOLIC HEAD

The aim here is to take a face and make it into a decorative image. I used a photograph of a friend of mine which is clearly defined and full-face. I divided all the areas of the features in such a way that I could put decorative patterns across them, rather similar to those which a tattoo artist might make. It creates an interesting and sometimes arresting image.

STEP 1

Find a good photograph of a face and draw it lightly to start with in order to get the shapes of the features in the right place and the right size. If your photo is large enough you could do it by tracing around the main shape and features.

STEP 2

Now draw in the shape more accurately in a firm single line. Make the hair more interesting by drawing various waves and curls wreathing up off the top of the head. The hair need not be too naturalistic, because here we are making a series of decorative patterns rather than a portrait.

STEP 3

Now comes the fun part when you divide the areas of the face and hair into a series of shapes to circulate around the facial features, almost like a set of tattoos. At this stage just stick to the larger shapes which divide the face in an interesting way.

STEP 4
Now really go to town and divide all these larger shapes into more and more decorative and detailed patterns.

Symbolic drawing

As on pp. 70–71, here I've shown a group of drawings that are inspired by very different traditions, but are very similar in style.

Heraldic eagle

This eagle from an old German heraldic image designed for an imperial banner is typical of the medieval method of showing images that remain in the memory. Its wings, legs and claws are displayed to give maximum effect to view.

SUN FACE

I chose an image from the pre-Columbian art of the Aztec Empire and added further facial features which are slightly more like the images from Indian banners. I felt the two styles could be put together with great effect.

HEART SHAPES

This image is culled from various sources, one of which is the traditional images used in European folk art. It could be used for St Valentine's Day cards.

ABSTRACT AND NATURALISTIC FORMS

The next three exercises use forms that are all based on reality but abstracted to a certain degree to make them easier to design. The whirlwind could be quite naturalistic, but here is turned into a decorative shape; the second exercise is based on plants and simple geometric forms mixed up together, while the third exercise uses purely geometric images. I have used tone to give a more three-dimensional effect to the images, so that they have a bit more depth and solidity to them.

THE WHIRLWIND

This drawing is of a vast whirlwind arising from the sea. More formalized than realistic, it creates an interesting spiral shape that appears to be very large and made up of natural forms.

STEP 1

First draw a curving rounded spiral, thin at the base and increasing in width as it rises up to the top of the space. At this stage keep it lightly drawn and vague in detail.

STEP 2

In the next stage you can draw in more precisely the shapes of waves and spray around the main shape of the whirlwind, which should have a narrow twisting base opening out to a hollow funnel shape looking like water and foam. At this stage use thin, more precisely drawn lines.

STEP 3

Next, put in tone all over the background, against which the drawn shapes can stand out. When you have shaded it with your pencil, rub it over with a paper stump (tortillon), which will make the tone look more solid and set off the main shapes nicely.

STEP 4

The last phase is to put in more tones on the main shape of the whirlwind, showing the darker areas along the sides to give it a rounded look and leaving all the areas of cloud and foam white. Adding a little darker tone on the white clouds around the spout will give them a more rounded shape. Now you have a large whirlwind rising out of a stormy sea.

Nature and geometry combined

The fun in making a drawing like the one shown here is to be completely guided by your own ideas, adding as many shapes as will help to fill up the space in a decorative way. Be guided by your own sense of design and although your drawings may not always come out exactly as you might have hoped, it will be fun seeing how well you can make the shapes hang together to create an attractive piece of artwork.

STEP 1
For this picture, start off with a careful outline drawing of a flower-like shape somewhere near the centre of the page.

STEP 2
Then add some leaf shapes around it, a bowl of rounded shapes above and behind it, a few pyramid shapes to one side and an extended stalk of fat rounded shapes. Draw some long curved shapes that could look naturalistic shooting off from the blossom and bowl.

STEP 3
In the next stage, add
other shapes curving around
the ones already there, some
like flames and others like leaves.

STEP 4

Now put in some
shading to give an
effect of depth to
the many shapes drawn.
Vary the darkness of the
tone, using your judgment to
decide where to make it lighter or
darker. The result will be an abstract three-
dimensional pattern of shapes that are partly geometric
and partly naturalistic. Each time you try this exercise
you will discover a new form of abstract patterning.

SOLID GEOMETRY

This piece has many geometric shapes that are drawn and shaded to look as three-dimensional as possible.

STEP 1

Begin by loosely drawing cubes, spheres, cylinders, pyramids, cones and even some polygonal shapes. Cluster them together as though they are all placed on a surface.

STEP 2

Now draw them in more accurately in a firm single line that defines each shape precisely. It may take you a bit of time to get all the shapes as exact as you can, but persevere as the finished effect will look more impressive.

STEP 3

Put in a tonal area on the side of the apparent objects, being consistent about the direction of the light. I have chosen the upper left-hand side to be the source of light. Keep all this tone uniform and fairly light.

STEP 4

Now work over the areas where you consider
that the darkest shadow will appear, so that
the shapes start to take on a more realistic
effect. Don't forget to put in some cast
shadows to the right of the objects.
The more carefully you draw
this tone the more solid the
geometric shapes will look.

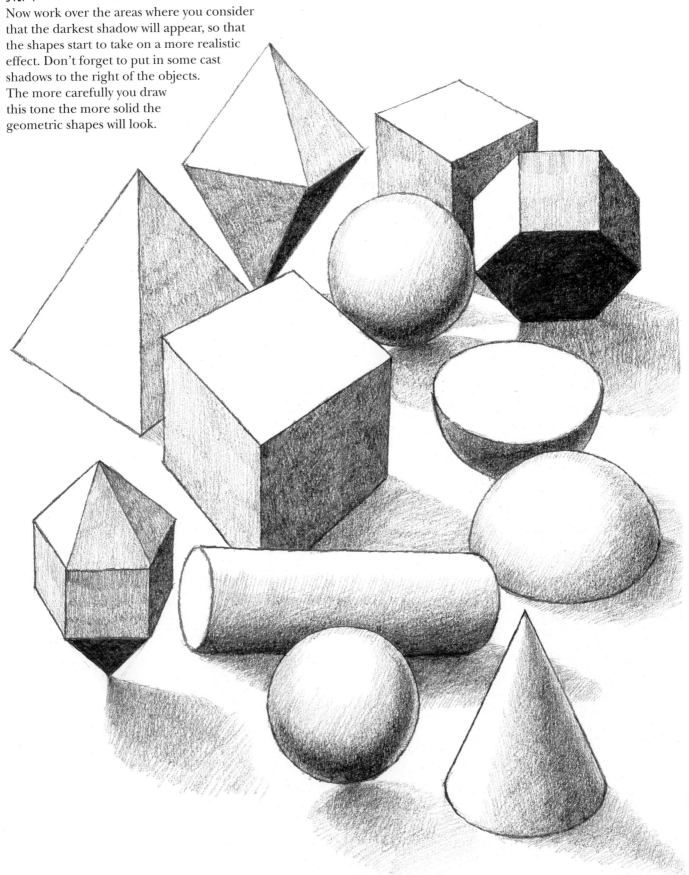

FISH IN THE SEA

In this last drawing I have returned to a natural theme, pulling together the symbolic and decorative styles we have looked at in the book.

STEP 1

You will first have to decide on some fish and shell shapes, then practise drawing them separately until you feel you have got them right. As these are all going to be combined in the same drawing, keep the size and number limited.

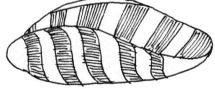

STEP 2

Now trace them down on to your main sheet of paper and around them draw curves that look like watery shapes. Draw some bubbles coming from the fish.

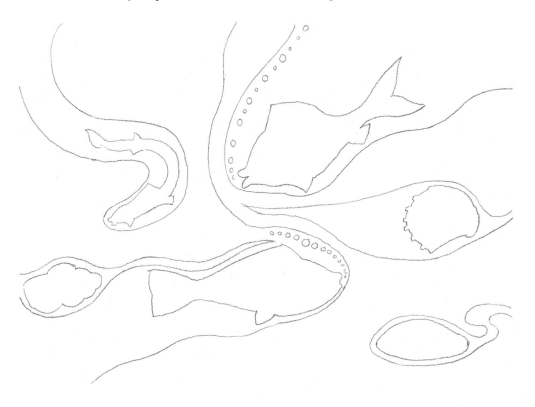

STEP 3

Take the curved shapes a stage further, drawing them as watery patterns around the fish and shells.

STEP 4

Finally, draw in the details of the fish and shells, then put in some tonal areas to give the whole drawing more solidity and depth.

Keep drawing mindfully

The practice of mindful drawing is designed not only to help your drawing abilities but also to give you a chance to calm your mind and give your attention to just one thing, which is enormously restful. Draw for a little while each day, or as often as possible, as it will act as a still point between all the other activities that keep you constantly on the go. In this way you will give your mind a period of repose that will bring you the benefit of greater energy and enthusiasm for life.